Veggies

by Christopher Michaelson

Veggies are so good for you.

They're colourful and bright, it's true!

They come in many shapes and sizes,

sometimes full of fun surprises.

There are zesty peppers and leafy greens,

crunchy carrots and sweet green peas.

Creamy avocados and juicy tomatoes,

Asparagus and baked potatoes!

They're full of nutrients and vitamins.

That help your body grow and shine.

So don't be afraid to try them out.

They're a tasty way to dine.

So the next time you see a veggie plate,

take a moment to appreciate,

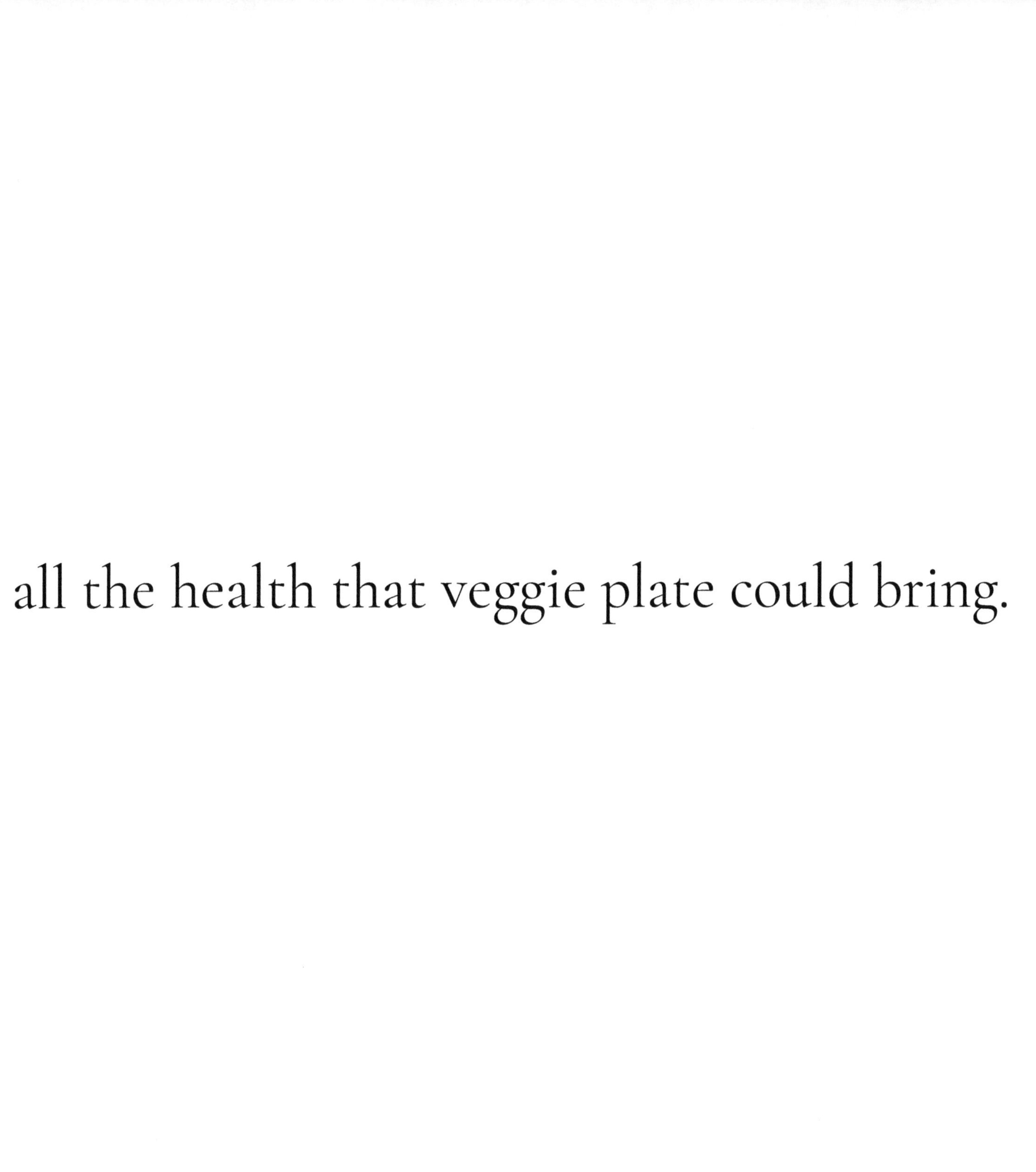

all the health that veggie plate could bring.

It's a great way to try some tasty things!

More books at
www.christophermichaelson.com